WORLD-WIDE GUIDE TO
GAY NUDE RESORTS, BEACHES AND RECREATION

1995–96

Second Edition

SUMMERS EDGE STUDIOS, INC.
757 S.E. 17th Street, Suite 307
Fort Lauderdale, FL 33316
(305)764-6162

Copyright © 1995 by Summers Edge Studios, Inc.

All rights reserved. Published in the U.S.A. by

Summers Edge Studios, Inc.

ISBN 1-887895-00-0

No part of this publication may be reproduced or transmitted in any form or by any means, electronic or mechanical, including photocopying, recording, or by and information storage or retrieval system, without permission in writing from the publisher.

The listing of any individual's name, business, group or organization in this guide, or any photograph, does not indicate or imply their sexual orientation is homosexual, nor does it indicate or imply that they encourage or discourage patronage by homosexuals.

FORWARD TO THE 1995–96 EDITION

This is the second edition of the World-Wide Guide to Gay Nude Resorts, Beaches and Recreation. This edition provides not only more listings, but also more information for gay nude enthusiasts. We have provided listings of naturist/nude organizations and how to get into contact with them for memberships and naturist newsletters, tips on making plans for your nude trips, names of nude publications providing loads of tid-bits from political views to recipes to changing anti-nudity laws by state, a listing of specialty travel groups and a travel agent to assist in making travel arrangements. To sum it up, this second edition is your complete travel partner in nude fun.

Much of the information contained in this guide has been assembled from individuals with local knowledge of a particular area and a lot of attention has been given to verifying the accuracy of information provided. Conditions can change, however, including the enactment or enforement of anti-nudity laws. the editor and publisher are not responsible for the enactment or enforcement of any laws, errors in the information provided, or for changes in ownership or desired patronage of any business listed in this guide.

This Guide should be treated as an information source rather than as a infallible reference book.

We welcome comments about the information and listings in the guide and we are always interested in receiving information on new beaches, destinations, accommodations or other items of interest.

CONTENTS

BEACH ETIQUETTE	2	CANADA	41
UNITED STATES		Ontario	41
Alabama	3	Quebec	43
Arizona	3	MEXICO	44
Arkansas	4	AUSTRALIA	44
California	5	New South Wales	44
Colorado	15	Northern Territories	46
Connecticut	15	Queensland	46
Delaware	16	South Australia	48
District of Colombia	16	Victoria	48
Florida	16	Western Australia	50
Georgia	23	COSTA RICA	51
Hawaii	24	AUSTRIA	51
Illinois	26	BARBADOS	51
Iowa	26	BRAZIL	52
Louisiana	26	DENMARK	52
Massachusetts	27	FINLAND	53
Michigan	28	FRANCE	54
Montana	29	GERMANY	55
Nevada	29	GREECE	56
New Hampshire	30	GUADELOUPE	57
New Jersey	30	HONG KONG	58
New Mexico	31	INDONESIA	58
New York	31	IRELAND	59
Ohio	33	ISRAEL	59
Oregon	34	ITALY	59
Pennsylvania	34	MARTINIQUE	60
Rhode Island	35	NEW ZEALAND	60
South Carolina	35	NORWAY	61
Tennessee	36	PORTUGAL	62
Texas	36	RUSSIA	62
Vermont	38	SINGAPORE	62
Virginia	38	SPAIN	63
Washington	38	THAILAND	65
Wisconsin	39	UNITED KINGDOM	65
Puerto Rico	40	Information of Interest	67
U.S. Virgin Islands	40	Taking a Nude Trip	67
CANADA	41	Tours and Travel	69
British Columbia	41	*Naked* Magazine	70
Nova Scotia	41	Nudist Organizations	71

INTRODUCTION

Gay nude recreation is a major growth industry for the 1990's. The number of clothing optional resorts is steadily increasing, and many resorts that are not completely clothing optional allow nude sunbathing and swimming. At some gay accommodations, the idea of nude sunbathing is assumed; so much so, that it's not even mentioned in the accommodation's promotional literature.

Gay travelers who are looking for a clothing optional vacation or trip, however, want to be assured their expectations will be met. This Guide has been published to provide the information needed to plan a trip that includes nude activity.

When making a reservation or trip plan, it is best to confirm with the accommodation that its policy towards nudity hasn't changed. Similarly, it is wise to enquire locally to ensure that neither the anti-nudity laws nor the enforcement of them have changed. Perhaps the best rule of thumb is to not be the first person to take off your clothes in an unfamiliar public place unless you are certain nudity is acceptable.

If you do find a gay nude beach or organization, or a accommodation that allows nudity, and that isn't listed here, please let us know.

The beaches listed here are those that are either gay or that have a mixed (straight/gay) use. There are hundreds of more nude beaches around the world that are primarily heterosexual. A book listing most of the world's nude beaches can be purchased from The Naturist Society at (414) 231-9977.

Discover the experience of nude hiking and other outdoor activities at some of the locations listed in *World-Wide Guide To Gay Nude Resorts, Beaches & Recreation.*

Clothing-Optional Beach Etiquette and Pointers

- ✓ **Stay Out Of Dunes** and other environmentally sensitive areas.

- ✓ **Don't Go Out Of Established Nude Areas.** To wander nude in a clothed beach or parking area may offend others.

- ✓ **Obey Parking Regulations** and other posted rules.

- ✓ **Help With Litter** by bringing along a trash bag. Carrying out more than you brought in.

- ✓ **Respect The Property Of Others.**

- ✓ **Ask Prior Consent For Photography.**

- ✓ **Privacy Is Fundamental.** Many are at club or beach for quiet time. Body language should tell you they don't want to be disturbed. It's not wrong to look for new friends - but it's rude to intrude when you're unwelcome.

- ✓ **Come Prepared.** Bring beach supplies: beverages, food, chairs, sunscreen and a towel.

- ✓ **Respect Others Sexual Orientation.** Don't assume that everyone on the beach is gay. Many nude beaches attract others from all walks of life and beliefs. Know in advance what to expect at the beach you plan to visit.

- ✓ **Speak Up For Standards.** If a person seems unaware of beach etiquette, explain it, kindly and plainly. Don't let others ruin the freedom you enjoy at nude beaches.

- ✓ **Be Friendly and Have Fun.** You never know who you may meet and having fun will help you make new friends.

UNITED STATES of AMERICA

ALABAMA

Birmingham

K. R.
P. O. Box 55244
Birmingham, AL 35255

Gay male nudist group

ARIZONA

Glendale

Arrowzona Private Casita
P.O. Box 11253
Glendale, AZ 85318
(602) 561-2300

Gay male guest house with nudity permitted in pool/spa area. Full breakfast and Health Club included. Located NW of Phoenix.

Phoenix

ANDES
(Arizona Nude Dudes)
P.O. Box 32776
Phoenix, AZ 85064-2776
(602) 274-1474

Gay nudist group.

Arizona Royal Villa
1110 East Turney
Phoenix, AZ 85014
(602) 266-6883

Apartment/Suites for gay men. Close to valley bars. All rooms with full accomodations. Nudity permitted.

Arizona Sunburst Inn
6245 N 12th Place
Phoenix, AZ 85014
(602) 274-1474

All male Bed & Breakfast resort. Caters to gay male naturists. Private yard, pool and hot tub. Clothing optional facility. Centrally located, close to local bars.

Flex Complex
1517 S. Black Canyon Hwy
Phoenix, AZ 85009
(602) 271-9011

Health club for gay men. Overnight accommodations available. Nude sunbathing permitted at poolside. Membership required.

Westways Resort Inn
P. O. Box 41624
Phoenix, AZ 85080
(602) 382-3868
(602) 263-7761

A private resort. The clientele is mostly gay men with women welcome. Some straight guests. Nude sunbathing permitted at swimming pool and sunbathing area. The entire resort can be clothing optional if it is booked by a single group. Six rooms with private baths. Swimming pool, Jacuzzi, exercise facility; massage available.

Tucson

ANDES
(Arizona Nude Dudes)
P.O. Box 64044
Tucson, AZ 85728-4044

Gay nudist group.

ARKANSAS

A.B.S. (Arkansas Bare Society)
Route 8, Box 264-A
Mountain Home, AR 72653
(501) 481-5415

Fayetteville

Flat Rock — Nude recreation area

Take State Route 16 past Durham. When you enter Madison county, take the first road to the left and follow it across the river to a metal gate; this is private property, but the owner doesn't mind. (Don't block the gate or park in the road). After the gate, walk through two pastures to the footbridge leading to the rocks.

CALIFORNIA

Auburn

American River — Nude swimming area
Take I-80 north to the Elm Ave. Exit. Drive east on Elm Ave. Turn left on Highway 49 (High Street). Go about 2 miles to an area where there is parking space on both sides of the road. Look for the trail heading towards the river.

Guernerville - see Russian River/Guernerville

Lake Tahoe

Sierra Wood Guest House
P. O. Box 11194
Tahoe Paradise, CA 95708
(916) 577-6073

Guest house for gay men and women only. Nudity permitted on sun deck and by pool.

Los Angeles

Compound
5636 Vineland Ave.
N. Hollywood, CA 91601
(818) 760-6969

Health club for gay men. Nude sunbathing permitted on sun deck. Private club.

Coral Sands Hotel.
1730 N. Western Ave.
Los Angeles, CA 90027
(213) 467-5141
(800) 421-3650
(800) 367-7263 (in CA)

Hotel with mostly gay clientele. Nude sunbathing permitted on sun deck and poolside. Fifty-eight rooms with private baths, swimming pool, Jacuzzi and sauna.

Flex
4424 Melrose Ave.
Los Angeles, CA 90027

Health club and spa for men only. Large outdoor pool where nude sunbathing and is permitted.

H.A.N.G.
P.O. Box 26881
Los Angeles, CA 90027

(Hosting All Nude Gays). Gay or bisexual men group hosting nude males visiting other areas. Membership US$15. Send SASE.

6 UNITED STATES

L.A.N.G.
P. O. Box 93434
Los Angeles, CA 90093-0434
(818) 377-2692

(Los Angeles Nude Gays). Gay male nudist group.

Roman Holiday
12814 Venice Blvd.
W. Hollywood, CA 90066
(213) 397-9091

Health club for gay men. Nude sunbathing permitted on sun deck. Private club.

Roman Holiday
14435 Victory Blvd.
Van Nuys, CA
(818) 780-1320

Health club for gay men. Nude sunbathing permitted on sun deck. Private club.

San Vicente Inn
845 San Vicente Blvd.
W. Hollywood, CA 90069
(310) 854-6915

A resort with gardens, pool, spa and sundecks. Clothing optional facility. Large rooms overlooking pool. Cottages available. Walking distance from bars and dining.

Monterey

Garrapata Beach   Nude beach

Take Highway 1 south from Monterey about 9 miles past Rio Road. At the bridge over the Garrapata river look for a stone house above the cliff. Park near the bridge. You can get to the beach by descending the 20' cliff on dirt steps to the riverside. The north end of the beach is mostly gay.

Mountain View

Barely Social
P.O. Box 726
Mountain View, CA 94042

Gay male naturist club.

Palm Springs

Alexander Resort
598 Grenfall Rd.
Palm Springs, CA 92262
(619) 327-6911

Guest house for gay men only. Entire resort is clothing optional. Eight rooms, all with private baths. Swimming pool and Jacuzzi. Continental breakfast and light lunch served daily.

UNITED STATES 7

Aruba Hotel Suites
671 South Riverside Drive
Palm Springs, CA 92262
(619) 325-8440
(800) 84-ARUBA

Condominium style one and two bedroom suites for men and women. Nude sunbathing permitted. Swimming pool and Jacuzzi.

Atrium
981 Camino Parocela
Palm Springs, CA 92262
(619) 322-2402
(800) 669-1069

Resort for gay men only. Entire resort is clothing optional. Private patios, one and two bedroom suites, fireplaces, swimming pool, Jacuzzi and exercise facilities.

Avanti Resort Hotel
715 San Lorenzo Road
Palm Springs, CA 92264
(619) 325-9723
(800) 572-2779

Resort for gay men. Secluded clothing optional resort. Large pool and spa area. Daily continental breakfast. Spectacular mountain view. Fun, friendly staff.

The Brambles
68-369 Sunair Rd. C.C.
Palm Springs, CA 92262
(619) 324-1350
(800) DESERT-5

Two and one-half acre clothing optional resort. Continental breakfast. Within walking distance of popular clubs and restaurants.

Cabana Club Resort
970 Parocela Place
Palm Springs, CA 92262
(619) 320-1300
(800) 669-WARM

Resort. Mostly for gay men with women welcome. Nude sunbathing permitted. Swimming pool.

Camp Palm Springs
722 San Lorenzo Rd. P.S.
Palm Springs, CA 92262
(619) 322-CAMP
(800) 793-0063

Pool and 16-man spa area are clothing optional.

Canyon Club
960 N Palm Canyon Dr.
Palm Springs, CA 92262
(619) 322-4367

32 Rooms & Suites. Steam room & Sauna Large pool & spa. Clothing optional. Walk to downtown.

The Columns
537 Grenfall Rd.
Palm Springs, CA 92264
(619) 325-0655
(800) 798-0655

Resort hotel for gay men only. Entire facility is clothing optional. Seven rooms with private baths and kitchens. Swimming pool and Jacuzzi.

8   UNITED STATES

Desert Paradise Hotel
615 Warm Sands Drive.
Palm Springs, CA 92264
(619) 320-5650

Resort for gay men. Discreet nude sunbathing permitted. Swimming pool and Jacuzzi.

El Mirasol Villas
525 Warm Sands Drive
Palm Springs, CA 92262
(619) 325-7191
(800) 327-2985

Resort for gay men and women. Nude sunbathing permitted. Swimming pool and Jacuzzi

The "550"
550 Warm Sands Drive.
Palm Springs, CA 92264
(619) 320-1744

Hotel for gay men only. Entire facility is clothing optional. Six rooms with private baths. Swimming pool and Jacuzzi.

Le Garbo Inn
287 W. Racquet Club
Palm Springs, CA 92262
(619) 325-6737

Resort for men and women. Nude sunbathing permitted. Swimming pool and Jacuzzi.

Hacienda en Sueno
586 Warm Sands Drive.
Palm Springs, CA 92264
(619) 327-8111
(800) 359-2007

Resort for gay men only. Nude sunbathing permitted. Swimming pool.

Harlow Club Hotel
175 E. El Alameda
Palm Springs, CA 92262
(619) 323-3977

Resort for gay men only. Nude sunbathing sunbathing permitted on sun deck. Swimming pool and Jacuzzi.

Inn Exile
960 Camino Parocela
Palm Springs, CA 92264
(619) 327-6413
(800) 962-0186

Resort for gay men only. Entire resort is clothing optional. Nine rooms and suites. Swimming pool and Jacuzzi. Continental breakfast and full lunch served daily; happy hour. A true desert luxury resort

Inn Trigue
526 Warm Sands Drive.
Palm Springs, CA 92264
(619) 323-7505

Resort for gay men only. Entire resort is clothing optional. Seven rooms and suites. Swimming pool and Jacuzzi. Daily continental breakfast and happy hour.

Inntimate
556 Warm Sands Drive
Palm Springs, CA 92264
(619) 778-8334

Resort for gay men only. Nude sunbathing permitted. Swimming pool and Jacuzzi.

UNITED STATES 9

Mirage
555 Grenfall Rd.
Palm Springs, CA 92264
(619) 322-2404
(800) 669-1069

Resort for gay men only. Entire resort is clothing optional. Swimming pool and Jacuzzi. Advertised as "The Most Unique Resort in the Desert."

Monaco Villa Resort
371 Camino Monte Vista
Palm Springs, CA 92262
(619) 323-3233

Resort for men and women. Discreet nude sunbathing permitted. Swimming pool and Jacuzzi.

P.S.S.S.T.
Palm Springs Social Sun Tanners)
P.O. Box 767
Palm Springs, CA 92263
(619) 325-5815

Gay male naturist club.

Santiago
650 San Lorenzo Rd.
Palm Springs, CA 92264
(619) 322-1300
(800) 710-7729

Resort for gay men only. Entire resort is clothing optional. Twenty-three distinctively designed rooms many with kitchen facilities. Magnificent panoramic mountain view. Expansive private grounds with oversized swimming pool and spa. Guest laundry facilities. Complimentary buffet style breakfast, luncheon, video library and Golds Gym passes.

Triangle Inn
555 San Lorenzo Rd.
Palm Springs, CA 92264
(619) 322-7993

Resort for gay men. Discreet nude sun bathing permitted. Swimming pool and Jacuzzi.

Vista Grande Villa
574 Warm Sands Drive.
Palm Springs, CA 92264
(619) 322-2404
(800) 669-1069

Resort for gay men only. Entire resort is clothing optional. Swimming pool and Jacuzzi.

Whispering Palms Hotel
545 Warm Sands Drive.
Palm Springs, CA 92264
(619) 320-1300
(800) 669-WARM

Resort. Mostly gay men with women welcome. Entire resort is clothing optional. Swimming pool and Jacuzzi

Inn Exile - The Ultimate Palm Springs Resort

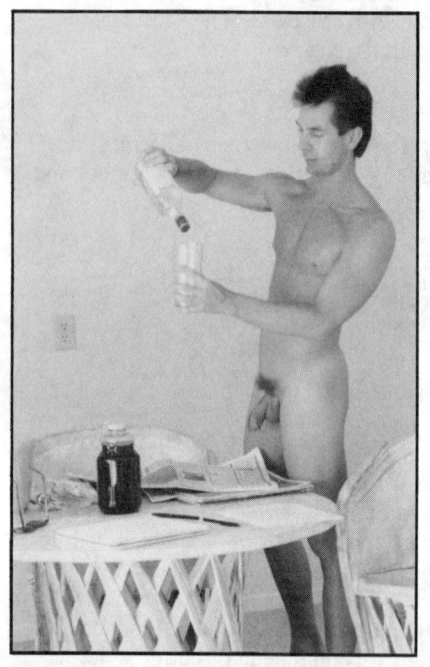

One of the best resorts in Palm Springs is Inn Exile - a luxury resort with true clothing optional ambiance. The Inn offers nine plush rooms and suites, a well-landscaped pool area, a heated Jacuzzi available for use 24 hours a day and a reputation for pampering its guests. It also has an exercise room for those who want to keep in shape while on vacation.

The hosts have made every effort to provide the little extras that add to a stay. The rooms all have TV's, VCR's and a rotating stock of adult male films. One of the nicest extras is a seemingly never ending supply of huge towels.

Continental breakfast, a full lunch and an afternoon happy hour are provided daily. Single travelers will enjoy the chance to meet other guests during meals and happy hour.

Pismo Beach

B.C.B.
(Bare Coast Boys)
P.O. Box 868
Pismo Beach, CA 93448
(805) 481-9161

Gay male naturist club.

Redding

Clear Creek Nude swimming area

From Redding head west-south-west on Placer Street. (I-16) towards Igo. Placer Street will become Placer Road. Park near the bridge over Clear Creek and follow the trail on the left side of the creek.

Redwood City

Edun Cove Nude beach (Also called Devil's Slide)

From San Francisco, take Highway 1 south about 5 miles past Pacifica. Look for Devil's Slide, a large cliff that drops off to the sea. Park at the marked "Beach Parking" area.

Russian River/Guernerville

Fife's
16467 River Road
PO Box 45
Guernerville, CA 95446
(707) 869-0656

Classic country resort for gay men, women and straight clientele. On Russian River surrounded by forests and meadow. Nude sunbathing area. Seasonal hours/call for information.

Highlands Resort
1400 Woodland Drive
(Mail: P. O. Box 346)
Guernerville, CA 95446
(707) 869-0333

Resort for gay men and women. Nudity permitted at swimming pool and hot tub areas. Sixteen rooms; ten with private bath.

The Willows
15905 River Rd.
(Mail: P. O. Box 465)
Guernerville, CA 95446
(707) 869-3279

Resort for gay men and women. During the summer months most of the guests are men. Nudity permitted in enclosed sunbathing area and in sauna and hot tub. Fourteen rooms. The resort is on the river and it offers canoeing and other activities.

12 UNITED STATES

Woods Resort
16881 Armstrong Woods Rd.
(Mail: P. O. Box 1690)
Guernerville, CA 95446
(707) 869-0111

Resort for gay men and women. Nude sunbathing permitted.

Wohler Bridge   Nude beach

From San Francisco take Highway 101 north past Santa Rosa. Turn left on River Rd. and then turn right on Wohler Rd. Park in the lot near the bridge and walk to the sandy beach about 1 mile upstream.

San Clemente

San Onofre Beach State Park   Nude Beach

San Onofre Beach, just south of the San Onofre nuclear power plant, is used by straights and gays. Take the Basilone Road Exit from I-5 and head towards the nuclear plant. Continue south to the park entrance ($6) and park at Trail Head No. 6. The nude beach is to the south - towards Camp Pendleton.

San Diego

B.B.C.
(Bare Buns of California)
P.O. Box 34361
San Diego, CA 92163
(619) 239-NUDE

Gay male naturist club.

Blacks Beach   Nude Beach

One of the most popular and well-known nude beaches in the country. The northern end is generally considered to be the gay section but straights and gays seem to use the entire beach with harmony. Blacks beach is north of San Diego, near the Torrey Pines glider port. Take I-5 north from San Diego to the Genessee Ave. Exit. Go west on Genessee through the first light where Genessee becomes North Torrey Pines Road. Go 1/2 mile and turn right onto Torrey Pines Scenic Drive. At the sign for the glider port turn left on the road leading to it. The parking area is 300 feet above the beach; look for a path leading to a steep set of rough stairs down to the beach. On most days, peddlers hawk soft drinks and beer along the beach.

UNITED STATES 13

Silver Strand State Beach   Nude Beach

From San Diego, take I-5 to the Coronado Cays exit. Follow the signs to the park.

San Louis Obispo

Pirates Cove   Nude beach

Take the Avila Beach Exit from Highway 101 and head west for 2 miles on Avila Rd. Look for a golf course on the right, and a bluff and 10 large oil storage tanks on top of a hill. Then look for a blacktop road marked with a sign "Not a Through Road - No Overnight Camping." Take the road for about 1/4 mile to a parking area.

San Francisco

G.M.N.   Gay male naturist club.
(Gay Male Nudists)
P. O. Box 14175
San Francisco, CA 94114-0175
(415) 974-9446

G.N.E.B.   Gay male naturist club.
(Gay Naturists East Bay)
584 Castro Street, #151
San Francisco, Ca 94114

SKiNs   Gay male naturist club.
(San Francisco Kindred Nudists)
P.O. Box 192492
San Francisco, CA 94119-2492

Angel Island   Nude Beach

Angel Island, in San Francisco Bay, is a popular day trip. During the summer, the fog reaches it later than most parts of the bay. The island is reached by State Park ferries. Perries Beach, which is clothing optional, is a 45 minute walk from the dock.

14 UNITED STATES

> **Bakers Beach** Nude beach
>
> Take Lincoln Blvd. to Bowley St. and then to Gibson Rd. At the west end of Gibson, walk towards the Golden Gate Bridge (north) down to the beach and then walk further north to Baker Beach. Frequented by both straights and gays.
>
> **Lands End Beach** Nude Beach
>
> Take Geary Blvd. to Point Lobos Avenue to Marine Way to Seal Rocks State Beach.

San Jose

Water Garden Health club for gay men. Nude sunbathing
1010 The Alamena permitted on garden sun deck. Membership
San Jose, CA required.
(408) 275-1215

San Mateo County (just south of San Francisco)

> **San Gregorio Beach** Nude Beach
>
> A popular beach that can often be cooled by fog during the summer months. From San Francisco, take Highway 1 south. Go 11 miles south of Half Moon Bay and look for the intersection of Highways 1 and 84. One hundred yards north of the intersection, on the beach side, is a dirt road leading to a white gate with the sign "Toll Road." Pay the fee ($2) and park. The parking area is privately owned. A trail heads down to the beach; walk north to the gay section. The gay section has a variety of log "enclosements" that early arrivals claim for the day.

Santa Cruz

B.B.B. Gay male naturist club.
(Bayside Bare Boys)
P.O. Box 7070
Santa Cruz, CA 95061

Sausalito

Bill Jones Houseboat Accommodations for gay men. Sunbathing
B-61, Issaquah Dock permitted on roof deck.
Sausalito, CA 94965
(415) 332-2270

COLORADO

Breckenridge

The Bunk House
P. O. Box 6
Breckenridge, CO 80424
(303) 453-6475

Resort for gay men only. Nudity permitted in the bunkhouse.

Denver

DAN-Ds
(Denver Area Nude Dudes)
P.O. Box 300193
Denver, CO 80203-0193

Gay male naturist club.

Denver Swim Club
6923 East Colfax
Denver, CO 80220
(303) 321-9399

Clothing optional facility, pool, weight room, lockers and rooms for rent. Minimal yearly membership required.

Vail

Mutz & Molly's B&B
P. O. Box 1384
Vail, CO 81658
(303) 476-7148

Bed and breakfast for gay men and women. Nude sunbathing allowed on sun deck. Six rooms; five with private bath.

CONNECTICUT

Hartford

B&G
(Bare and Gay of Connecticut)
P.O. Box 380264
East Hartford, CT 6138
(203) 569-4337

Gay male naturist club.

Norwalk

G.N.I.
(Gay Naturist International)
324 Main Street, Suite 201
Norwalk, CT 06851

Gay male naturist club.

DELAWARE

Rehoboth Beach

Rams Head Inn
RD2, Box 509
Rehoboth Beach, DE 19971
(302) 226-9171

Bed & breakfast for gay men only. Nudity permitted outdoors in fenced area, sauna and hot tub. Seven rooms; five with private baths. Continental breakfast, open bar from 4:30 to 6:00 pm, comfortable social area.

DISTRICT OF COLUMBIA

Lambda Soleil
P.O. Box 9635
Washington, DC 20016-9635

Gay male naturist club.

Club Washington
20 "O" Street SE
Washington, D.C. 20003
(202) 488-7317

Health club for gay men with nude sunbathing area. Membership required.

Devonshire House
7281 Lee Highway
Washington, D.C. 22042
(703) 533-0874

Bed and breakfast. Mostly women with men permitted. Nudity permitted at poolside.

FLORIDA

Amelia Island

Sea Kindly
999 1st Coast Hwy
West Amelia Island, FL 32034
(904) 378-8360

Private cruises on a charter sailboat. Nudity permitted at some anchorages.

Boca Raton

G.C.B.S.
(Gold Coast Bare Skins)
% J.J. Szukala
9690 Lancaster Place
Boca Raton, FL 33434-2743

Gay male naturist club.

Ft. Lauderdale

Big Ruby's Guest House
908 NE 15th Ave.
Ft. Lauderdale, FL 33304
(305) 523-RUBY

Gay Guest house. Mostly men with women welcome. Nude sunbathing area, swimming pool. Eight rooms; all with private bath.

Club Fort Lauderdale
400 West Broward
Ft Lauderdale, FL 33312
(305) 525-3344

Health club with outdoor swimming pool and nude sun deck. Membership required.

Kelly's Guesthouse
1909 S.W. 2nd Street
Ft Lauderdale, FL 33312
(305) 462-6035

Hidden in down-town Fort Lauderdale. Large nude pool area, sundecks, in a Key-West style guest house.

Midnight Sea
3106 Alhambra St.
Ft. Lauderdale, FL 33304
(305) 463-4827

Small motel with nude sunbathing area and straight and gay clientele.

The Palms on Las Olas
1760 East Las Olas Blvd.
Ft. Lauderdale, FL 33301
(305) 462-4178
(800) 550-POLO

Gay men hotel/resort. Nude sunbathing decks. Heated pool, BBQ. Waterfront locale. Spacious, lush secluded gardens. Thirteen rooms total, efficiencies, hotel rooms and suites available.

Jacksonville

F.C.N.J.
% Francisco
6801 Sans Souci Road
Jacksonville, FL 32216-4525

First Coast Naturist Jaybirds Gay male naturist club.

Key West

Alexander's
1118 Fleming St.
Key West, FL 33040
(305) 294-9919

A Guest house with mostly gay men and women as clientele. Nude sunbathing and swimming permitted. Ten rooms; eight with private bath.

Big Ruby's
409 Applerouth Lane
Key West, FL 33040
(305) 296-2323

A Guest house with mostly gay men with women welcome. Nude sunbathing and swimming permitted. Thirteen rooms; six with private bath. Lagoon-like swimming pool.

Big Ruby's - A Key West Style Guest House in Fort Lauderdale

Big Ruby's has become an institution in Fort Lauderdale. It offers pleasant surroundings at affordable rates. It also has a garden-style pool area for nude sunbathing and swimming. The pool area is a great place to meet other guests.

The guest house has eight rooms, each with its own bath. The poolside rooms have large window doors that open to the fresh air. During the season, morning coffee and donuts are served at the poolside cabana.

Big Ruby's is close to many of Fort Lauderdale's gay bars and other gay attractions.

UNITED STATES 19

Blue Parrot Inn
916 Elizabeth St.
Key West, FL 33040
(305) 296-0033
(800) 231-BIRD

Gay friendly Inn with heated swimming pool Nude Sundeck and Continental breakfast.

The Brass Key
412 Frances Street
Key West, FL 33040
(305) 296-4719
(800) 932-9119

A gay Guest house for men. Nude pool are for sunbathing. Full breakfast. All rooms furnished w/ AC, TV, refrigerator and include turndown service nightly.

Coconut Grove
817 Fleming St.
Key West, FL 33040
(305) 296-5107

Bed and breakfast for gay men only. Nudity permitted on sun deck and in swimming pool. Fifteen rooms; thirteen with bath, five suites.

Colours
The Guest Mansion
410 Fleming St.
Key West, FL 33040
(305) 294-6977

Guest house with mostly gay men and women clientele. Nudity permitted on sun deck and in swimming pool. Twelve rooms; ten with private bath, garden, exercise room, Jacuzzi.

Coral Tree Inn
822 Fleming Street
Key West, FL 33040
(305) 296-2131
(800) 362-7477
(Opens Dec. 21, 1992)

Guest house for gay men only. Entire facility is clothing optional. Eleven rooms, all with private bath and balconies, swimming pool and Jacuzzi. Complimentary expanded continental breakfast buffet and sunset wine and hors d' oeuvres.

Curry House
806 Fleming St.
Key West, FL 33040
(305) 294-6777

Bed and breakfast for gay men only. Nudity permitted on sun deck and in swimming pool. Eight rooms, six with private bath.

Cypress House
601-F Caroline St.
Key West, FL 33040
(305) 294-6969

Bed and breakfast for gay men only. Nudity permitted on sun deck and in swimming pool. Fifteen rooms, three with private bath.

Early House
507 Simonton St.
Key West, FL 33040
(305) 296-0214

Resort for gay men only. Nudity permitted in swimming pool, sun deck and Jacuzzi area. Eight rooms with shared bath.

UNITED STATES

Island House for Men
1129 Fleming St.
Key West, FL 33040
(305) 294-6284
(305) 292-0051/FAX

Guest house for gay men only. Entire facility is clothing optional. Thirty-six rooms, twenty-eight with private baths, swimming pool, sauna, Jacuzzi, work out center.

Lime House
219 Elizabeth St.
Key West, FL 33040
(305) 296-2978
(800) 374-4242

Guest house for gay men only. Entire facility is clothing optional. Nine rooms; seven with private baths, swimming pool, sun deck, Jacuzzi. Continental breakfast.

The Mermaid & The Alligator
729 Truman Ave.
Key West, FL 33040
(305) 294-1894

Bed and breakfast with straight and gay clientele. Nude swimming and sunbathing permitted. Eight rooms, five with private bath.

Newton Street Station
1414 Newton St.
Key West, FL 33040
(305) 294-4288
(800) 248-2457

Guest house for gay men only. Entire facility is clothing optional. Seven rooms; four with private bath, swimming pool, exercise facilities. Continental breakfast.

Oasis, A Guest house
823 Fleming St.
Key West, FL 33040
(305) 296-2131
(800) 362-7477

Guest house for gay men only. Entire facility is clothing optional. Nineteen rooms; seventeen with private bath., two swimming pools, Jacuzzi and sun deck. Complimentary expanded continental breakfast buffet and sunset wine and hors d'oeuvres.

The Pines
521 United St.
Key West, FL 33040
(305) 296-7467
(800) 282-7463
(305) 296-3928/FAX

Guest house for gay men and women only. Nudity permitted in pool and sun deck area. Fourteen rooms; all with private bath, beer and wine bar poolside.

Sea Isle Resort
915 Windsor Lane
Key West, FL 33040
(305) 294-5188
(800) 995-4786
(305) 296-7143/FAX

Resort for gay men only. Nudity permitted in swimming pool and sun deck areas. Twenty-four rooms; all with private bath, swimming pool, Nautilus gym, Jacuzzi, and private garden.

UNITED STATES 21

The Southwinds
1321 Simonton St.
Key West, FL 33040
(305) 296-2215

Motel with mostly gay (men and women) clientele. Nude sunbathing permitted in the pool and sun deck area.

GAY MEN'S SAILING

 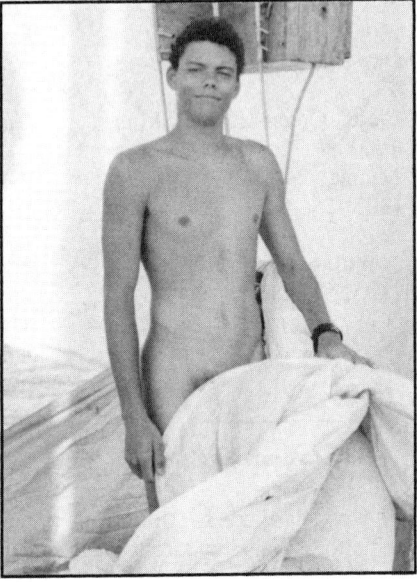

C L I O N E
"Butterfly of the Sea"

The Largest Gay-Owned and Operated Sail Charters in Key West! A day on the water designed specially for Gay Men. Six hour reef trips with all the equipment and instructions provided. Free stretch limo service also provided. The *Clione* is an excellent way to relax on the beautiful waters nude. Enjoy sailing, reef snorkling, swimming, or go along just for the experience. $70 per person and large groups can be accommodated. Call 296-1433 or 745-4519 for more information about this exciting sail boat experience.

Miami

Club Body Center
2991 Coral Way
Miami, FL
(305) 448-2241

Health club for gay men. Outdoor pool with nude sunbathing area. Overnight accommodations available. Membership required.

European Guest House
721 Michigan Ave.
Miami Beach, FL 33139
(305) 673-6665
(305) 672-7442/FAX

Bed and breakfast for gay men and women. Nudity permitted on deck and in garden area only. Thirteen rooms; nine with private baths, Jacuzzi.

Gold Coast Bare Skins
1000 NE 72nd Terrace
Miami, FL 33138
(305) 756-5434

Gay male nudist group

Normandy South
(305) 674-1197

Guest house for gay men only. Clothing optional. Five rooms; all with private bath, Jacuzzi, heated swimming pool with lap lane. Lush tropical grotto with secluded romantic hot tub for private times.

Haulover Beach Nude beach

A popular nude beach in Miami area for years. Take Collins Ave, (A1A), north of Bal Harbourt, through underpass. Straight and gay beach, gay area is the northern section of nude beach.

Orlando

GNOMES
(Gay Nude Orlando Men's
Enthusiasts Society)
3331 Danny Boy Circle
Orlando, FL 32808

Gay male naturist club.

St. Petersburg

Garden Geusthouses
920 4th Street South
St. Petersburg, FL 33701
(813) 821-3665

Gay male guest house. Swimming pool All rooms have full kitchenette, private bath. Nude sunbathing decks.

Tampa

Southern Exposure　　　Gay male naturist club.
P.O. Box 8092
Tampa, FL 33674-8092
(813) 985-4331

T.A.M.E.N.　　　Gay male naturist club.
(Tampa Area Men Enjoy Nature)
9403 Hartts Drive
Tampa, FL 33617-5226
(813) 985-4331

Titusville

Canaveral National Seashore　　　Nude beach

An attractive Central Florida beach with a designated section for naturists. The beach is for straight and gays, however the far northern section of the nude beach area you'll find a number of gay men sunbathing.

GEORGIA

Atlanta

The G.A.N.G.　　　Gay male nudist club.
(Greater Atlanta Naturist Group)
P. O. Box 7546
Atlanta, GA 30357

I.M.E.N.　　　Gay male naturist club.
(International Men Enjoying
Naturism)
P.O. Box 77122
Atlanta, Ga 30357
(404) 876-3064

Savannah

C.E.N.　　　Gay male nudist club.
(Coastal empire Naturists)
119 Old Dock Road
Savannah, GA 31410

HAWAII

Hawaii Island

A.O.K.K.
(Aikane O Ke Kohana)
P.O. Box 15385
Honolulu, HI 96830-5385
(808) 735-4114

Gay male naturist club.

Kalani Honua Beach & Ranch Retreat
P. O. Box 4500
Kalapana Beach, HI 96778
(808) 965-7828

Bed and breakfast with a straight and gay clientele. Nude sunbathing permitted on the beach and, at night only, in the spa.

R.B.R Farms
P. O. Box 930
Captain Cook, HI 96704
(808) 328-9212

Guest house with mostly gay male clientele. Gay women welcome. Nudity permitted on common deck, pool area and in gardens. Five rooms, one with private bath, swimming pool. Full breakfast served daily.

Honokohau Harbor   Nude beach

An attractive and often photographed beach popular with both straights and gays. The beach is north of Kailua and south of the Kailua-Kona airport. Head towards the ocean on the Honokohau Harbor Road. Bear right until the road dead ends just past the Kona Marina; follow the main road around the marina. Look for a sign pointing to the beach and "NB" painted on rocks. The beach has a gay section.

Kauai

Vacation Rental
Call Thomas at
(808) 828-1626

Two bedroom vacation rental unit located five minutes from Secret Beach.

Mahina Kai
4933 Aliomanu Rd.
P. O. Box 699
Anahola, Kauai, HI 96703
(808) 822-9451

Guest house for gay men and women. Clothing optional, but most nudity occurs around pool area and private patios off each room. Five rooms with private baths swimming pool and Jacuzzi.

Royal Drive Cottages
147 Royal Drive
Kapaa, Kauai HI 96746
(808) 822-2321

Cottages located in the green hills above Sleeping Giant Mountain. Private drive, secluded in the Wailua district.

Donkey Beach   Nude beach

A crescent shaped beach popular with both straights and gays on the east coast of Kauai. Take Route 56 north from Kapaa toward Anahola. Watch for a cane plantation road on the right after the 11 mile-marker and just before the 12 mile-marker. Take the cane road and bear right. Donkey Beach will be 1/2 mile on the left.

Secret Beach   Nude beach

A beautiful beach protected by a 300 foot cliff. Take route 56 northwest from Kapaa to Kilauea. Just after the 23 mile marker, turn sharply right at the Shell station. Go 100 feet and turn left onto Kilauea Rd. From the Shell station, go 1.35 miles to Kauapea Rd. on your left. A steep path winds down to the beach.

Maui Island

Camp Kula
Kula, Maui, HI 96790
(808) 878-2529
(808) 878-2529/FAX

Bed and breakfast for gay men and women. Clothing optional garden and sun deck. Five bedroom estate on seven acres.

Hana Plantation Houses
P. O. Box 489
Kihlei, Maui, HI 96713
(808) 248-7248
(800) 657-5723

Rental apartments with straight and gay clientele. Nude sunbathing allowed on sun deck.

The Triple Lei
P. O. Box 593
Kihlei, Maui, HI 96753
(808) 874-8645

Guest house with mostly gay male clientele; lesbians welcome. Entire facility is clothing optional. Swimming pool.

Maui Island

Little Makena Beach   Nude Beach

A great beach located on the sunny region of Maui. Good body surfing. The beach is located at the end of Route 31. One mile past the Maui Prince Hotel turn right onto a rough road to the parking area. The nude beach is to the right of the lava flow.

ILLINOIS

Chicago

C.A.N.S. Gay male naturist club.
(Chicago Area Naturist Sons)
3023 N. Clark Street, #367
Chicago, IL 60657

W.C.G.N. Gay male naturist club.
(Windy City Gay Naturists)
P.O. Box 2547
Chicago, IL 60690

IOWA

Des Moines

I.B. Naturist Club
(Iowa Bareskins)
P.O. Box 266
Des Moines, IA 50301-0266
(515) 270-2954

Eldridge

G-MEN Gay male naturist club.
(Gay Men Enjoying Nudity)
% J. Peters
301 N. 5th Street
Eldridge, IA 52748-1124
(319) 285-4375

LOUISIANA

New Orleans

Ursuline Guest House Hotel for gay men only. Nudity allowed in
708 rue des Ursulines whirlpool area.
New Orleans, LA 70116
(504) 525-8509

MASSACHUSETTS

Boston

B.A.N.G.
(Boston Area Naturist Group)
P.O. Box 2191
Boston, MA 02118-0036
(617) 695-8113

Gay male naturist club.

Revere Beach — Nude Beach

Gay male nude beach. Just 2 miles north of Boston Downtown, on the boulevard between Band Sand and Kelly's. Take the blue line to Revere Beach or Wonderland Station.

Chicopee

G.S.G.N.
(Greater Springfield Gay Nudists)
1981 Memorial Drive, Suite 146
Chicopee, MA 01020
(413) 534-1053

Gay male naturist club.

Provincetown

Brass Key Guesthouse
9 Court St.
Provincetown, MA 02657
(617) 487-9005
(800) 842-9858

Bed and breakfast for gay men and women. Garden and sun deck are clothing optional. Fifteen rooms with private baths. Jacuzzis. All rooms w/ refrigerator, luxury amenities.

Carl's Guest House
68 Bradford St.
Provincetown, MA 02657
(508) 487-1650
(800) 348-CARL

Very popular. Guest house for gay men with clothing optional sundeck. Close walk to gay bars. 14 guest rooms with private baths.

Gabriels
104 Bradford St.
Provincetown, MA 02657
(508) 487-3232

Guest house with mostly lesbian clientele; gay men welcome. Hot tub and sun deck are clothing optional (for women only)

28 UNITED STATES

Normandy House
184 Bradford St.
Provincetown, MA 02657
(617) 487-1197

Guest house for gay men. Nude sunbathing allowed.

Herring Cove   Nude Beach

Mostly gay beach just outside of Provincetown. Can be reached by walking, biking or by car. Parking is available is National Park Service lot ($6).

Truro Beach   Nude beach

Located on Route 6 between Ballston Beach and Long Nook Beach. Popular with both straights and gays.

MICHIGAN

Ann Arbor

Sunshine Partners, Inc.
P.O. Box 2191
Ann Arbor, MI 48106-2191
(313) 665-6363

Gay male naturist club.

Saugatuck/Douglas

The Kirby House
294 West Center
P.O. Box 1124
Douglas, MI 49453
(616) 857-2904

Guest House for gay men and lesbians. Nudist Area. Breakfast included. Good local.

Saugatuck Lodges
6492 Blue Star Hwy.
Saugatuck, MI 49453
(616) 857-4269 (summer)
(312) 929-0001 (winter)

Resort for gay men only. Nude sunbathing allowed on the grounds.

Oval Beach County Park Nude Beach

The nude area is north of the public area. Very popular with gays. Check locally for the current enforcement climate.

**Saugatuck Dunes
State Park** Nude Beach

The beach is north of Saugatuck on the Blue Star Highway. Look for signs to the Michigan Dunes Correction Facilities; follow them until you come to the Saugatuck Dunes State Park signs and parking lot. The nude area is about a mile north of the public area. Check locally for the current enforcement climate.

MONTANA

Ronan

North Crow Ranch
2360 North Crow Rd.
Ronan, MT 59864
(406) 676-5169

Campground for gay men and women.

NEVADA

Las Vegas

Sun Runners
P.O. Box 72189-GN
Las Vegas, NV 89170

Gay male naturist club.

Las Vegas Bed & Breakfast
(702) 384-1129

Guest house for gay men. Entire guest house is clothing optional. Three bedrooms and two baths.

Lake Meade Rec. Area Nude Beach

Take Lake Mead Blvd. south to dead end. Turn left and drive 4.7 miles to 8.0 road and turn right. From there, take all left hand turns on the gravel road. Park, then walk east to the beach.

NEW HAMPSHIRE

Bath

Evergreen Bed & Breakfast
U.S. Route 302
Bath, New Hampshire 03740
(603) 747-3947

Gay only guest house in large antique home. Nudity permitted in hot tub room, bar area and outside sunbathing area. Located near the beautiful Ammonoosuc River.

NEW JERSEY

Bloomfield

N.J.B.
(New Jersey Bares)
P.O. Box 482
Bloomfield, NJ 07003
(201) 656-1249

Gay male naturist club.

Gateway National Recreation Area/Highlands

Sandy Hook — Nude Beach

Probably the most popular nude beach for the Middle Atlantic States. Large gay following. Take the Garden State Parkway to Exit 117; then take Route 36 east to Sandy Hook (about 12 miles). At Sandy Hook, follow signs to North Beach. Park in lots G or H near the Old Gun Battery (about five miles from the park entrance. The nude area is about 1/4 mile south (along the beach) of the parking area.

Voorhees

P.A.N.G.
(Philadelphia Area Naked Guys)
1105 Cooper Court
Voorhees, NJ 08043-1812
(609) 772-9336

Gay male naturist club.

NEW MEXICO

Albuquerque

Dave's B & B
PO Box 27214
Albuquerque, NM 87125
(505) 247-8312

Close to Old Town.

Santa Fe

SFBBB
(Santa Fe Bare Buns & Balls)
% Gregg Watkins
7548 Kachina Loop
Santa Fe, NM 87505

Gay male naturist club.

NEW YORK

Lake Placid

> **Cooperas Pond**   Nude Beach
>
> Take Highway 86 north for about 5 miles from the intersection of Highways 73 and 86. A trail on the east side of the road leads to the woods and pond.

New York City

M.A.N.
496-A Hudson St., Suite 133
New York, NY 10014
(212) 535-3914

Males Au Natural. Gay male nudist group. All of the clubs activities are conducted in the nude.

Colonial House Inn
318 W. 22nd St.
New York, NY 10011
(212) 243-9669
(212) 633-1612/FAX

Guest house for gay men and women. Nude sunbathing permitted on rooftop sun deck. Nineteen rooms; seven with private bath.

Hotel 17
225 E. 17th St.
New York, NY 10003
(212) 475-2845
(212) 677-8178/FAX

Hotel with straight and gay clientele. Nude sunbathing permitted on sun deck (limited). An artsy, budget hotel with 160 rooms; all with shared baths.

New York City/Fire Island

Cherry Grove and
Fire Island Pines — Nude beaches

Highly popular nude beaches with largely gay use. Fire Island is a low slung barrier reef south of Long Island. It can only be reached by ferry, or perhaps by private boat or charter seaplane.

Point O'Woods — Nude beach

Not quite as gay as Cherry Grove or Fire Island Pines. Clothed and unclothed sunbathers generally coexist without any problems.

New York City/Long Island

Jones Beach — Nude beach

A popular beach with straights and gays. Take the Meadowbrook Parkway south to Jones Beach. Park in Field 6 and walk east along the beach for about 30 minutes to the nude area.

New York City/Staten Island

White Pickets
67 Brewster St.
Stapleton, NY 10204
(718) 727-9398

Bed and breakfast with straight and gay clientele. Large fenced yard for nude sunbathing

Rochester

H.U.N.G.
(Hosting Upstate Nude Guys)
P.O. Box 92293
Rochester, NY 14692
(716) 624-9337

Gay male naturist club.

Sayville

Cherry Grove Beach Hotel and Ice Palace
PO Box 537
Sayville, NY 11782
(516) 597-6600

Accessable by ferry only.

OHIO

Cincinnati

S.O.N.S.
(Southern Ohio Naturist Society)
% C. Turner, 2115 Fulton Ave, #E
Cincinnati, OH 45206
(513) 861-2201

Gay male naturist club.

Cleveland

Club Body Center
1448 West 32nd Street
Cleveland, OH 44113
(216) 961-2727

Health club with nude sun deck. Overnight accommodations available. Membership required.

Columbus

M.O.O.N.
(Mid-Ohio Organization of Naturists)
P.O. Box 164141
Columbus, OH 43216

Gay male naturist club.

Rockbridge

O.G.N.A.
26500 Wildcat Rd.
Rockbridge, OH 43149
(614) 385-6822

(Ohio Gay Naturists Assoc.) Gay male nudist group associated with Summit Lodge Resort.

Summit Lodge Resort
26500 Wildcat Rd.
Rockbridge, OH 43149
(614) 385-6822

Clothing optional Guest house and campgrounds. Straight and gay clientele. Swimming pool, 400 acres of grounds.

Youngstown

G.E.N.T.
(Gentlemen Enjoying Nudity Together)
% Mac, P.O. Box 3902
Youngstown, OH 44513

Gay male naturist club.

OREGON

Portland

Sauvie Island Game Refuge — Nude beach and recreation area

Used by both gays and straights. From Portland, take Highway 30 north to the Sauvie Island Bridge. Take Reeder Road for about 4 miles past Social Security Beach. Watch for two trails leading to the river.

Rogue River

Whispering Pines
9188 W. Evans Creek Rd.
Rogue River, OR 97537
(503) 582-1757
(800) 788-1757

Bed and breakfast with large gay following. Nude swimming and sunbathing allowed in pool and sun deck area.

PENNSYLVANIA

Gibson

Hillside Campgrounds
P. O. Box 726
Binghampton, NY 13902
(717) 756-2833

Campgrounds for gay men only. Nudity allowed throughout the grounds. Campsite facilities include: all sites with electric/water hook-up, small cabins, RV units for rent, storage lockers and camp store.

New Milford

Oneida Camp
P. O. Box 537
New Milford, PA 18834
(717) 465-7011

Campgrounds and guest house for with mostly gay men as clientele. Lesbians welcome. Entire camp is clothing optional. Twelve rooms and cabins, sauna and clubhouse. Small membership fee required.

Philadelphia

G.L.N.
P. O. Box 2239
Philadelphia, PA 19103

Gay & Lesbian Naturists

RHODE ISLAND

Pawtucket

R.I.N.G.
(Rhode Island Naturist Group)
P.O. Box 1384
Pawtucket, RI 02862
(401) 722-2416

Gay male naturist club.

Providence/South Kingston

Moonstone Beach — Nude beach

A nude beach used by both straights and gays. Take Route 4 from I-95. It will become Route 1 after a traffic circle. Exit at the sign for Trustom Pond National Wildlife Refuge (a U-Turn will be required) onto Moonstone Beach Road. You can park (for a fee) at Roy Carpenter's Beach.

Westerly

Misquamicut State Beach — Nude beach

Located approximately 6 miles south of Moonstone Beach.

SOUTH CAROLINA

Charleston

Charleston Beach Bed & Breakfast
118 West Arctic Ave.
P. O. Box 41
Charleston, SC 29439
(803) 588-9443

Guest house for gay men and women. Nude sunbathing allowed in enclosed courtyard. Nine rooms; two with private baths. Near nude beach.

36 UNITED STATES

Charleston

Edisto Island Nude beach

Take I-95 to Waterboro, then take Highway 64 to US 17, then Route 174. The nude section is 1-2 miles north of the parking area.

Folly Beach Nude beach

Park at the Folly Beach parking area (fee charged). Walk right, around the end towards the Intercoastal Waterway.

TENNESSEE

Greenville

Timberfell Lodge
Rte. 11, Box 94A
Greeneville, TN 37743
(615) 234-0833
(800) 437-0118

Guest house for gay men only. Entire facility is clothing optional. Swimming pool with beer bar, Jacuzzi, exercise room. Fourteen rooms; two with private baths. Private, well-screened resort with 250 acres to roam nude on.

Rogersville

Lee Valley Farm
Rte. 9, Box 223
Rogersville, TN 37857
(615) 272-4068

Guest farm with cabins. Mostly gay male clientele; gay women welcome. The owner says nudity is allowed "just about" anywhere except in the dining room. Swimming pool, hot tub, hiking and a whole farm-full of other outdoor activities including fishing and horseback riding. Six rooms; two with private baths.

TEXAS

Austin

A.G.N.
(Austin Gay Nudists)
P.O. Box 684101
Austin, TX 78766-4101
(512) 451-5951

Gay male naturist club.

Austin

Lake Travis
Hippy Hollow — Nude beach

A popular nude beach with a separate gay section. Take Highway 2222 from Austin for 15 miles. Turn left onto Highway 620. Turn right at the Comanche Trail, "Hippy Hollow County Park" sign. Park in the first lot on the left (fee charged). Gays gather at the far end. Caution - don't dive from the limestone ledges as the bottom is very irregular.

Dallas

M.A.N.
4315 Holland, # 106
Dallas, TX 75219
(214) 276-0387

Metroplex Assoc. of Nudists

Jp's Place in Dallas
515 North Marsalis
Dallas, TX 75203
(214) 941-5640

Sauna, Exclusive for Gay Men

Houston

L.S.N.G.
(Long Star Nudist Group)
P.O. Box 54061
Houston, TX 77254
(713) 880-2261

Gay male naturist club.

South Padre Island

Lyle's Deck
120 E. Atol
(Mail: P. O. Box 2326)
South Padre Island, TX 78597
(512) 761-5953

Guest house for gay men and women only. Nude sunbathing and nude beach area. Fourteen rooms; thirteen with private bath. One suite. Swimming pool, Jacuzzi and exercise facility.

San Antonio

BEXAR Men
P.O. Box 12342
San Antonio, TX 78212-0342
(512) 341-5400

Gay male naturist club.

VERMONT

Putney

Mapleton Farm
Bed & Breakfast
Rte. 2, Box 510
Putney, VT 05346
(802) 257-5252

Guest house with mostly gay clientele. Near two nude beaches. Nudity also allowed in wooded part of property. Eight rooms; three with private bath.

Shaftsbury

Country Cousin
Old Depot Rd.
Rt. 1B, Box 212
Shaftsbury, VT 05262
(802) 375-6985

Bed and breakfast with mostly gay clientele. Nude sunbathing allowed. Five rooms; two with private baths, swimming pool and hot tub.

VIRGINIA

Arlington

Lambda Soliel
P. O. Box 5112
Arlington, VA 22205

Gay male nudist group

WASHINGTON

Olympia

Cooper Point Nude beach

Used by Evergreen State College students. Take Route 101/401 from I-5 to the campus. Take Cooper Point Drive to Driftwood and park in Lot F. Trail to the beach is at the rear of the lot. Bear to the right at each fork of the trail.

Olympia

J.H.
P. O. Box 1615
Olympia, WA 99209

Gay male nudist group

Seattle

The Olympians Gay male nudist group.
% T. Clements, 823 NE 80th St.
Seattle, WA 98116

Spokane

> **High Bridge/Peoples Park** Nude beach
>
> About a 15 minute walk from downtown Spokane. Head west on Riverside Avenue until Riverside intersects Clarke near the Spokane River. Walk about 400 yards the the forested area until you come to the parking lot near the junction of Hangman Creek with the Spokane River. The nude beach is located where Latah Creek joins the Spokane River.

WISCONSIN

Kenosha

W.B. Gay male naturist club.
(Wisconsin Bares)
P.O. Box 1684
Kenosha, WI 53141-1684
(414) 694-9559

Madison

> **Mazo Nude Beach** Nude beach
>
> On the Wisconsin River about 14 miles west of Madison in the Mazomanie State Wildlife Refuge. Take County Y for 4 miles and turn left on Laws Rd. The nude beach is near where the cars park. Canoes are available for rent locally for nude canoeing.

Wausau

M.E.N. Gay male naturist club.
(Men Enjoying Naturism)
% G.M.C., P.O. Box 2371
Wausau, WI 54402-2371

PUERTO RICO

San Juan

Ocean Park Beach Inn
3 calle Elena, Ocean Park
San Juan, PR 00911
(809) 728-7418

Guest house excluseively gay clientele. Nude sunbathing (discreet) allowed. Twelve rooms.

U.S. VIRGIN ISLANDS

St. Croix

Tin Roof Inn
P. O. Box 1818
Frederiksted
St. Croix, USVI 00841
(809) 772-1002
(809) 772-1188/FAX

Bed & breakfast for gay men and women. Nude swimming and sunbathing allowed. Twelve apartments, pools, sun deck, garden and balcony.

St. Thomas

The Mark St. Thomas
Blackbeard's Hill
Charlotte Amalie
St. Thomas, USVI 00802
(809) 774-5511
(809) 774-8509/FAX

Hotel with straight and gay clientele. Discreet nude sunbathing allowed. Eight rooms with private bath, two suites and one cottage.

The sensual freedom of swimming naked is one that we all should experience. The *World-Wide Guide to Gay Nude Resorts, Beaches & Recreation* is dedicated to helping you achieve that and much more.

CANADA

BRITISH COLUMBIA

Vancouver

P-CAN
P.O. Box 530
1027 Davie Street
Vancouver, BC V6E 4L2 Canada
(604) 732-6396

Pacific-Canadian Assoc. of Nudists.

Wreck Beach Nude beach

Canada's most popular nude beach with an active gay section. Take Marine Drive west off Highway 99. Watch for a Wreck Beach sign; there are several parking areas and trails down to the beach. The gay section is to the left along the beach.

NOVA SCOTIA

Halifax

Crystal Crescent Beach Nude Beach

Take Herring Cove Road from Halifax to Sambro Light House. Turn off onto Old Sambro Road directly across from light house. It is approximately 20 miles out of town on Herring Cove Road. Very scenic drive and road has many bends and curves. The predominately gay beach area is located behind sand dunes at the end of the beach.

ONTARIO

Grand Valley

Manfred's Meadow Resort
RR # 1,
Grand Valley, ONT L0N 1G0
(519) 925-5306

Guest house for gay men only. Entire resort is clothing optional. Eight rooms; four with private bath, swimming pool, hot tub, exercise facilities, sun deck and a sauna. All on a 100 acre farm.

Huntsville

Divine Lake Resort
RR1 Box XD3
Port Sydney, ONT P0B 1L0
(705) 385-1212
(800) 263-6600

Resort for gay men and women. Popular resort for fishing and hiking. Nude sunbathing on lake dock. Main resort clothing is required.

Ottawa

GO-NUTS
475 Elgin Street, #1711
Ottawa, ON K2P 2E6 Canada

Gay Ottawa Nudists Under The Sun.

The Stonehouse
2605-10th Line Rd., R.R. #1
Edwards, ONT K0A 1V0
(613) 821-3822

Bed and breakfast for gay men and women only. Nude sunbathing allowed in garden. Three rooms; one with private baths.

Toronto

T-CAN
Box 66, 552 Church Street
Toronto, ON M4Y 2E3 Canada
(416) 966-4944

Toronto Canada Area Naturists.

TANGO
Greenwin Square Postal Outlet
345 Bloor St. East
Toronto, Ontario M4W 3S9

Toronto Area Nude Guys Association

Seaton Pretty Bed and Breakfast
327 Seaton Street
Toronto, Ontario M5A 2T6
(416) 972-1485

Guest house for gay and lesbians. Nude sunbathing on the sundeck is permitted.

Muther's
508 Eastern Ave.
Toronto, Ontario M4W 3S9
(416) 466-8616

Guesthouse for gay men above Tool Box bar and restaurant. Nude sundecks.

Scarbourough Beach   Nude Beach

East of Warden Avenue. Mostly gay and most often nude. Ocassional police harrassment if nude so use your own judgement when visiting Scarbourough beach.

QUEBEC

Montreal

Auberge du Centre Ville
1070 rue Mackay
Montreal, QC H3G 2H1
(514) 938-9393
(514) 938-1616/FAX

Hotel and health club for gay men only. Forty-nine rooms; twenty-nine with private baths. Nudity permitted in sauna, garden and on sun deck.

La Conciergerie Guest House
1019 rue St. Hubert
Montreal, QC H2L 3Y3
(514) 289-9297
(514) 289-0845/FAX

Guest house for gay men only. Nudity permitted on roof-top sun deck and in Jacuzzi area. Seventeen rooms; nine with private baths.

Le St-Christophe Guest House
1597 St-Christophe
Montreal, QC H2L 3W7

Guest house for gay men only. Nudity permitted on sundeck. Rooms with private baths available. Jacuzzi. Full breakfast.

Cte. Yamasaka

Domaine Gay-Luron Enrg.
R.G. Grande Terrei
St. Francois-Du-Lac
Cte. Yamasaka, QC J0G 1M0
(514) 568-3634

Summer resort for gay men only

St. Alphonse De Granby

Bain de Nature
125 Lussier
St. Alphonse de Granby
QC J0E 2A0
(514) 375-4765

Summer resort for gay men only. Entire resort is clothing optional. Swimming pool, Jacuzzi. Three rooms, one with private bath.

St. Marthe

Camping du Plein Bois
550 Chemin St-Henri
St. Marthe, QC
(514) 459-4646

Gay men only campground and recreation. Nudity permitted. Dancing and swimming on premises.

MEXICO

Cancun

Yucatan Peninsula Nude beach

From Cancun, drive south on Highway 307 down the coast for 45 miles (65 km to Playa del Carmen. Walk north on the beach for 3 km. Just past second sandy point is the nude beach. Northern section of beach is predominatly gay. The beach is long and clean with palm trees and calm surf. A small reef makes for great snorkling. A great get away.

AUSTRALIA

No other country has beaches that equal those in Australia, especially in terms of sheer mileage and in numbers where nude swimming and sunbathing occur. "Free" beaches are usually designated as such and nudity is officially permitted. Beyond its free beaches, Australia has thousands of miles of beaches, much of which are often unvisited, particularly during the weekdays. If no one else is around, then almost any rural beach can become a nude beach.

At the more popular beaches, the gay section is generally at the farthest point away from the family areas.

NEW SOUTH WALES

Ballina

Shelly Beach Nude beach

A beautiful cove, located just north of Ballina, at the mouth of the Richmond River. Look for a paved road just after the first residential subdivision. The north end is usually used by nudists and gay men. Not an official nude beach.

AUSTRALIA 45

Northern Rivers (Byron Bay)

King's Beach   Nude beach

The main beach is popular with families. Just south ok Kings Beach are two secluded coves that are mostly gay. You can get to them at low tide by walking over the rocks between the coves. Wear sensible shoes for the trek over the rocks; it you try it bare foot or in thongs, it becomes a servival trip.

Sydney

S.S.B.   Gay male naturist club.
(Sydney Sunboys)
P.O. Box 1117, Bondi Junction
Sydney, NSW 2022 Australia

Governors on Fitzroy   Guest house with mostly gay male clientele,
64 Fitzroy St., Surry Hills   lesbians welcome. Nudity permitted on sun
Mail: P. O. Box 866   deck and spa area. Six rooms with shared
Darlinghurst, NSW 2010   baths.
(02) 331-4652
For reservations from U.S.
& Canada call (516) 944-5330

Free Beaches

Sydney has a number of free (nude) beaches, not all of which have a large gay following. The ones listed below do. The readers best option is to acquire a city map to mark out the beaches listed below, and then to ask locally to see if any changes have been made to the nudity regulations at a particular beach. Public transportation is available to most, but not all of the beaches.

Lady Jane   Nude beach

Located in Watson's Bay in the spectacular Sydney Harbor area and not on the ocean. It is officially nude and very popular with gay men.

Little Congwong Beach   Nude beach

The main beach, Congwong Beach, is popular with families. Little Congwong Beach is right next to it. It's not officially nude, but lots of the beachgoers are nude.

Sydney

Obelisk Bay Nude beach

Another harbor beach. Near Mosman in northeast Sydney. It's not officially nude, but it's small, it's mostly nude and it's popular with gay men.

Woodburn

All Gay Nudist Retreat
Box 108
Woodburn, NSW 2472
(066) 822-365

Completely clothing optional retreat for gays. Tent camping, one small cabin, or shared accommodations in a country house. Sauna.

NORTHERN TERRITORIES

Darwin

Casuarina Free Beach Nude beach

Nude sunbathing occurs at the northern end. Frequented by gay men. Swimming at Casuarina Beach isn't possible during the Australian summer (wet season) because of the highly poisonous jelly fish, called sea wasps or stingers, present. Their venom is among the most poisonous of all venomous creatures.

QUEENSLAND

Brisbane

Stradbroke Island Nude beach

Can be reached by taking the car ferry from Redland Bay, southeast of Brisbane. Once on the island, drive 6 km towards Mt. Van, the 4km further to Blue Lake Beach.

Cairns

Be Bee's
379 Mayers St.
P. O. Box 120
Edgehill, Cairns, QLD 4870
(070) 321-677/536-681/FAX

Resort complex for gay men and lesbians only. Nude sunbathing and swimming allowed. Pool, sun deck, Jacuzzi. Twenty rooms; six with private baths, ten suites.

Turtle Cove Resort
P. O. Box 158
Smithfield, Cairns, QLD 4878
(070) 59 1800

Resott complex for gay men and lesbians only. Located on private, clothing optional beach. Twenty rooms, all with private bath, dining room, pool, spa, sundeck, cocktail bar and mini-gym.

Buchans Point — Nude beach

An unofficial nude beach 25 kilometers north of Cairns. There have been reports of some police activity.

Yorkey's Knob — Nude beach

Located about 8 kilometers north of Cairns. The nude section is at the north end, near the rocks.

Hervey Bay

Rainbow Beach — Nude beach

For the adventurous. At the northern end of Cooloola National Park via the road to Tin Can Bay. Follow the signs to Wide Bay and Double Island Point. A 4WD is recommended.

Noosa Heads

Stardust Holiday Apartments
P. O. Box 656
Noosa Heads, QLD 4567
(074) 47 4647

Six one-bedroom apartments for gay men and lesbians only. Suitable for stays of one night or longer. Swimming pool. Nude swimming and sunbathing allowed.

48 AUSTRALIA

Noosa Heads

Alexandria Bay Nude beach

One of the most popular nude beaches in Queensland. Has a strong gay following. Tourist maps available in Noosa show the locations and access points.

Bribie Island Nude beach

Located about 50 kilometers south of Noosa Heads and east of Caboolture. Follow the signs to Bribie Island. Once you cross the bridge to the island, take the road to Woorim. Once you reach the beach, walk about 4 km north. There have been some reports of police activity.

SOUTH AUSTRALIA

Adelaide

Maslin Beach Nude beach

Legal nude beach popluar with gays. A beautiful beach 3 km's long, one of the best nude beaches in Australia. The nude area is the south end. About an hour drive south of the city. Go south, through Morphet Vale, on Main South Road for about 45 km. Turn right onto Sandpits Road, then left at next intersection. Go south for several kilometers, turn right onto Tuit Road, go past the Maslin Beach Caravan Park and poark in the clifftop parking area.

VICTORIA

Melbourne Area

All of the nude beaches listed on the following page are within 150 kilometers of Melbourne.

Anglesea

Point Addis　　　Nude beach

Part of the beach has recently been made a legal free beach. The nude area is north of the point and the gay section is at the far end. Take Great Ocean Road to Anglesea. The road to the beach is 2 km past the Bell's Beach turn-off.

Lorne

Cathedral Rock　　　Nude beach

An unofficial nude beach 125 km southwest of Melbourne. The beach is near Cinema Point off Great Ocean Road. Park in the car park.

Port Phillip Bay/Mt. Eliza

Sunnyside North Beach　　　Nude beach

A popular official nude beach on the Mornington Penninsula and the closest nude beach to Melbourne. The gay section is at the far end of the beach, towards Mt. Eliza. From Melbourne, take the Nepean Highway (Route 3) south. Eight km south of Frankston, look for the sign to Sunnyside Beach.

Sommers

Sommers Beach　　　Nude beach

An unofficial nude beach near the town of Sommers on Western Port Bay, about 75 km southeast of Melbourne. From the car park at the beach, follow the track down to the water and then walk along the beach for about 2 km, past the "Commonwealth Property" sign.

Torquay/Breamlea

Point Impossible Nude beach

A popular official nude beach. The gay section is at the end of the beach. Take Route 1 west from Melbourne through Geelong. Just outside of Geelong, and before Torquay, turn left on the road to Breamlea. Just before the end of the road, turn left to Black Gate Road, drive to the end and park.

WESTERN AUSTRALIA

Perth

Swanborne Guest House Luxurious guest house for gay men and
5 Myera Street lesbians only. Sundeck and sunbathing area.
Swanbourne, WA 6010 Close to gay nude beach. Four rooms,
((09) 349-1408 some with private baths.

North Swanborne Beach Nude beach

A popular beach with a long history of nude use. The gay section is away from the crouds. Stay out of the sand dunes behind the beach. The sand is extremely hot and the dunes are sometimes patrolled by highly poisonous snakes and by policemen. Take the Stirling Highway southwest from Perth, turn right at Eric Street and right again onto Marine Parade and follow the road to the car park. The nude area is about 300 meters north.

Rockingham

Warnbro Beach Nude beach

Some people say thia beach is officially nude, others say it's not. Either way, it gets a lot of nude use. It has clear water, gentle waves and a clean beach. The afternoon winds are usually strong, so most people visit in the morning. From Rockingham, take Safety Beach Road south, then fendham Street until you reach the Nor 3 car park. The nude area is 1 km to the south, at the far end of the beach.

COSTA RICA

San Jose

Colours
Address correspondence to:
P. O. Box 025216-1522
Miami, FL 33102-5216
(305)532-9341
(800) ARRIVAL

A guest house with mostly gay clientele. Nude sunbathing and swimming allowed. Ten rooms; three with private bath.

AUSTRIA

Vienna

Dechantlacke in der Lobau Nude beach

A gay nude beach. Take Bus 91 A from Vienna International Center to Restaurant Roter Hiasl, then 10 minutes walk.

Donauinsel Nude beach

Take Bus 33 B from Franz-Jonas-Platz to Uberfuhrstrasse, cross the "Jedleseer Bridge", then 500 m to the right.

Donauinsel »Toter Grund« Nude beach

A must visit for gay tourists. Very popular. Take bus 91 A to Steinspornbrucke. After crossing the bridge 500 m to the left.

BARBADOS

St. Joseph

Cattlewash Beach Semi-Nude beach

Discreet Nudity is possible at Cattlewash Beach. Use discretion. Beach is located along East Coast Road. Best part for gays is between holiday houses and Barclays Park.

BRAZIL

Fortaleza

Praia do Cumbuco — Nude beach

Nude beach area in the dunes at the far western end. One hour from the city, near Icarai.

João Pessoa

La Plage de La Batterie — Nude beach

A cruisy nude beach. Take the Nice Exit from RN 7. On the other side of town watch for a Shell Gas Station on the left. A small parking area is nearby. Cross the road and take a subway passage to the beach.

Maceió

Ilha do Coroa — Nude beach

In the city go across the river at Barra de Santo Antonio follow signs to beach area.

DENMARK

Århus

Den Permanente
Mariendal Havbakker
Ballehage (near Højbjerg)
Fløjstrup Stand — Nude beaches

Esbjerg

Houstrup Strand — Nude beach

Near Lønne. From the parking area walk 500m in direction of the nude beach. Mostly gay men and a very popular beach.

Faxe Ladeplads

Beach on the "Feddet" Nude beach

This popular beach is located by the inlet of APraesto Fjord; after the parking area there is a nudist beach, and further on the beach it will become more and more gay.

København

Tisvilde Strand Nude beach

Public beach in North Sealand. Go by train east to Hillerød, change to private railroad for Tisvildeleje. The beach is about 2 km from the station; pass park and go 1 to 2 km west. The beach will gradually get more and more nude and gay as you walk.

FINLAND

Helsinki

Seurasaari Nude beach

Turku

Ruissalo Saaronniemi Nude beach

Nudist beach is loacted behind the camping area on the Island of Ruissalo.

Turun Ulimahalli Nude beach

Men only beach and facility on Tuesdays, Thursdays and Saturdays. Very popular among local gays.

FRANCE

Agde

Plage Naturiste Nude beach

This beach is loacted between Marseillan-Plage and the nudist area found there.

Au Bois-Joli Nude beach and campground

Cannes

Praia da tambaba Nude beach

First official nude beach located in the northeast. Beach is located about 30 miles south of town. Popular, yet secluded as for specific directions.

Ile Sainte-Marguerire Nude beach

The east side, facing the Ile Saint-Honorat is clothing optional.

Plage de la Batterie Nude beach

Enter Cannes at Golfe-Juan, near the new service station.

Marseillan plage Nude beach

Between Sete and Cap d'Adge, you can reach this area by N312. Pass Cap d'Adge, the second street to the right. At the beach walk to the right and there you will find a huge gay nude beach.

Marseille

Le Mont Rose Nude beach

A cruisy nude beach. Take bus # 19 to the last station. Follow the boardwalk near the beach.

Nice

Jetee du Port — Nude beach

A nude beach with year round cruising. Take a path along the sea towards Cap de Nice. The nude beach is just beyond the Coco Beach Restaurant.

Toulouse

En Rose
32120 Solomiac
Toulouse 31000
6267-7248

Guest house for gay men only. Nudity permitted in pool and sun deck area. Four rooms and three apartments.

GERMANY

Berlin

Strandbad Wannasee — Nude beach

A lake beach with a sanctioned nudist area. Can be reached via the S-Bahn to Nikolassee Station.

Kronach

Schlasshotel Fischbach
Fischbach
96316 Kronach
(09261) 3006

Hotel for gay men. Nudity permitted in pool and sauna area. All rooms include televisions and telephones.

Westerland

Haus Hallig
Botticher Strass 3
2289 Westerlund-Sylt
(4651) 24-213

Guest house for gay men only. It is located only 20 minutes away from the nude beach at Westerlund. Eighteen rooms.

Kronach

Westerlund Beach — Nude beach

A beautiful nude beach with first class facilities. The nude section is a 45 minute walk south of the town.

GREECE

THE GREEK ISLANDS

Corfu

Myrtiotissa Beach — Nude beach

A mixed nudist (gay/straight) beach near Pelekas. Turn right off the main road at Pelekas and head towards Glyfadas. Look for a sign for Mrytiotissa and a wide lane through the tree on the left side of the road. Drive down the lane to a parking area. The parking area is on a cliff about 800 feet over the beach. A trail leads to the beach. If you don't fancy an 800 foot climb back to your car, rent a pedal-boat at Glyfadas Beach and pedal north around the headland. You'll arrive at Myrtiotissa Beach after about a 10 minute paddle.

IOS

Koumbara Beach — Nude Beach

The beach, north of the harbor, can be reached by a 20 minute walk west from Yialos.

Manganari Beach — Nude beach

Located on the south coast of the island, it can only be reached be boat from the sea.

Mykonos

Mykonos is a garden of nude gay beaches. **Paradise** and **Super Paradise** are the established beaches with **Super Paradise** being the more secluded and active of the two. **Panorama and Elia Beaches** also have a lot of gay nude use. The beaches can all be reached by boat from Plati Yalos Beach - a 10 minute bus ride from the center of Mykonos.

Paros

Monastiri — Nude beach

This beautiful gay beach is located on the Bay of Naoussa. Nudity is permitted and this beach can be cruisy on the left-hand side of the beach when facing the sea.

Rhodes

Faliraki Beach — Nude beach

A beautiful nude beach with mixed (straight/gay) use on the Isle of Rhodes. About 15 minutes by bus from Rhodes. Walk to your right when you arrive at the beach and go about 2 km along the beach to the third cove.

Samos

Tsamadou Beach — Nude beach

Mostly gay men. Beach is located near Kakkari village. You can reach the beach by taking a bus from Samos town.

Skiathos

Banana Beach — Nude beach

This nudist beach is located next to Kokounaries Beach. Public buses from town until you reach last stop. Walk right over a small hill and through an olive grove.

GUADELOUPE

The sunny islands of Guadeloupe offer some of the most heavenly beaches in the Caribbean. Some beaches have legal nudity established while other beaches have nudity; discretion is advised. The readers best option is to obtain information and directions from local gay friendly establishments. The following is a list of some of the more popular beaches where nudity can be found.

Guadeloupe

Pointe Tarare Nude beach

Located in Guadeloupe - St. Francois Pointe Tarare is a legal nudist beach.

Grande Saline Nude beach

Located in St. Barthelemy, Grande Saline has nude sunbathing, however it is not officially allowed, keep your wraps handy.

Cope Coy Nude beach
Orient Beach Nude beach

These two beaches are located in **St. Martin**. St. Martin is under the Guadaloupe jurisdiction. St. Martin is a beautiful paradise and is the perfect location for nature fans.

HONG KONG

Hong Kong Island

Middle Bay Nude beach

A very rocky swimming area at Repulse Bay. Take bus 320 or 6a from Central to Repulse Bay. Walk to southern part of beach. Nudity permitted between Middle Bay and South Bay.

INDONESIA

Bali

Bali spirit Hotel & Spa Hotel exclusively for gay men. Nudity is
(62) 361-9740 12 permitted at pool and terrace areas. Breakfast served daily. Hotel at end of Post Office Rd.

IRELAND

Dublin

"Forty Foot"	Nude beach
Dollymount	Nude beach
Beach is located at the far end of the sanddunes.	

ISRAEL

Tel-Aviv

Gaash Beach	Nude beach
Located about 25 kilometers north of Tel-Aviv near Kibutz Gaash. The beach is hidden behind sand dunes.	

ITALY

Genova

Pieve Ligure	Nude beach
A gay nude beach located about 100 yards from the Pieve Ligure Railway Station. The beach is a considerable distance from Genova - a rental car is needed to reach it as bus and train service are unreliable.	

Milano

Ticino Beach	Nude beach
Located left of the Vigevano Bridge. Not always nude but usually gay.	

Turin

Flume Orco — Nude beach

A gay beach along the MI-TO highway entrance at Chivasso. Nude during the summer months.

Venice

Lido Alberoni — Nude beach

A gay beach with frequent nudity.

MARTINIQUE
(Caribbean)

St. Anne

Anse Trabaud — Nude beach

Just before St. Anne, at the cross to go to Plage des Saline, take on the left of a private road for five km. There is a toll fee for FF 15. Once you have come to the beach area go 300 m to the right.

NEW ZEALAND

Auckland

Gentlemen's Bay — Nude beach

Gentlemen's bay is a gay nude beach close to St. Heliers Beach at the end of Tamaki Road. It is best for visitors to get directions.

Christ Church

Waimairi Beach — Nude beach

Waimairi Beach, also called North Beach, is a gay beach with frequent nudity. The gay section is to the north, particularly in the sand dunes behind the beach.

Nelson

The Hideaway
Lower Wangapeka
RD2 Wakefield
(054) 34-390

Country retreat for men only. Nude swimming and sunbathing allowed. Seven rooms; two with private baths, swimming pool and river beach.

Rotorua

Mount View Lodge
75 Mount View Drive
Rotorua
(073) 461-908

A guest house with mostly gay clientele. Nude sunbathing is allowed in garden and sun deck area. Four rooms with shared baths.

Wanganui

Uretiti Beach   Nude beach

To get to the beach, go onto the beach from the parking area and turn right.

NORWAY

Oslo

Gay Beach   Nude beach

Take bus 30 from downtown to lost stop at Bygdøy. Walk along the small path along parking lane on the right side you will find beach area. Mostly gay men some mixed crowds.

Porsgrunn

Olavsberget Camping/Beach   Nude beach

Olavsberget Camping by old E-18 in at the top of the hill in the forest behind the beach. Mostly gay.

PORTUGAL

Lisbon

Costa da Caparica — Nude beach

Costa da Caparica is a nude beach that may be becoming too popular with straight non-nudists. The beach is about 30 minutes south of Lisbon. The nude area is near # 19 beach. You can get to the beach by bus from Lisbon (Praca de Espanha), by ferry or by private car. If you are driving, cross the Telha (Tejo) Bridge and follow signs for Ponte de telha. Drive north to the end of the road behind the dunes.

RUSSIA

St. Petersburg

Sestroreck — Nude beach

A very popular all gay beach of St. Petersburg. Take the electric train for 30 minutes to Finland Railway Station. From station it is approximately a 30 minute walk by foot to nude beach. Worth the trip.

SINGAPORE

Sentosa Island — Nude beach

A popular mixed (straight/gay) nude beach. The gay section is near the golf course. Homosexuality is still punishable by life imprisonment in Singapore; caution is advised. Don't be the first one on the beach to go nude - or cruising.

SPAIN

Barcelona

Playa de Chernobil   Nude beach

Near Olympic City in S. Adrian de Besos. The beach is located behind the TAGRA-factory.

La Palma (Canary Islands)

Playa Los Cancajos   Nude beach

South of Santa Cruz. Mostly gay men of all ages. Walk along the beach from Los Cancajos to the south towards the airport. Climb over rocks (be careful) and walk for approximately 30 minutes until you reach the beach.

Playa Cuatro Monjas   Nude beach

South of Playa Naos. Mostly gay men of all ages. Follow road south just behind Puerta Naos. Park near banana plantations and you will see a path to the sea.

Maspalomas (Canary Islands)

Beach Boy Bungalos
Campo International
Gran Canaria

Resort complex for gay men only - near gay nude beach. The resort's swimming pool, poolside bar and sun deck are clothing optional. Twelve bungalows with private baths. Reservations can be made through Odysseus Tours - see Tour & Travel Section.

Los Robles
Campa de Golf
Maspalomas

Resort complex for gay men only - near gay nude beach. The resort's swimming pool poolside bar and sun deck are clothing optional. Twenty-one bungalows with private baths. Reservations can be made through Odysseus Tours - see Tour & Travel Section.

Maspalomas (Canary Islands)

Playa de Maspalomas — Nude beach

A popular nude beach close to town. The gay section can be reached via the Avenida de las Dunas by the lagoon.

Ibiza

Casa Alexio
Barrio Ses Torres 16
07819 Jesus, Ibiza
(71) 31.42.49

Guest house for gay men only. Nude swimming and sunbathing are allowed in the garden, pool and sun deck area. Ten rooms; eight with private baths.

Nude sunbathing is permitted everywhere outside of town and signs are posted reaching *Playa natural*, to show you the way to these beaches. The only main gay beachs located near Ibiza are listed below.

Es Cavallet/Las Salinas — Nude beaches

Both beaches are at Cabo Falcon - about 10 miles from Ibiza. The beaches can be reached by bus from Ibiza

Palma De Mallorca

Son gelabert Hostal
PO Box 107
07510 Sineu
(971) 52 02 47

Small guest house for gay men located deep in the countryside. It is a 30 minutes by car to Palma and Es Trench. Clothing optional facility with pool and breakfast served daily.

Es Trench — Nude beach

A very popular gay men's nude beach. Take road to Campos del Puerto, then go in the direction of Colonia de Sant Jordi. The beach is near El Ultimo Paraiso restaurant.

Playa Cala Guya — Nude beach

Gay area is located at the northern rocky part of the beach.

Sitges

Playa del Muerto — Nude beach

There are two nude beaches here; the farthest one is primarily gay. Take shuttle bus from the Cathedral to Golf Terramar. Then take the road to the old Guardia Civil Headquarters and walk along railway.

THAILAND

Pattaya

Jomtieh Beach — Beach

The beach gets some nude use by gays. Your accommodation can arrange transportation to the beach.

UNITED KINGDOM

Blackgang

Blackgang Chine — Nude beach

Mixed gay crowd. Walk along coast from St. Catherine Lighthouse about 2 km until you reach the beach. Walk along beach to far end below the cliffs area.

Bournemouth

Shell Bay — Nude beach

A mixed (stroight/gay) beach that can be reached via ferry from Sandbanks.

UNITED KINGDOM

Brighton

Brighton Beach   Nude beach

The official nude beach section is is 50 yards east of the main promenade near Peter Pan's Playground. It is marked by naturist signs.

London

G.N.G.   Gay male naturist club.
(Gay Nudist Group)
BM Box 5147
London, England WC1N 3XX U.K.

Gymnos 88   Gay male naturist club.
BM Box 372
London, England WC1N 3XX U.K.

L.G.N.   Gay male naturist club.
(London Gay Naturist)
BM 3377
London, England WC1N 3XX U.K.

Torquay

Cliff House Hotel   Gay and Lesbian resort hotel. Very popular
St. Marks Road   close to beach and to gay bars. All rooms
Meadfoot Beach   have private baths. Designated clothing
Devon TQ1 2EH   optional areas.
(01803) 29 46 56

INFORMATION OF INTEREST

Taking A Nude Trip

Maybe its something you've been dreaming about for a long time. And now the time has come – you want to take a nude vacation. Not just get nude every now and then, but be nude from the moment you arrive until the moment you depart. You can just picture it, a long, curving, palm tree-lined beach, the surf rolling in, a pleasant guest house perched on the beach's edge, other men to share it with and not a stitch of clothing in sight.

It all sounds nice. But unfortunately, clothing-optional, gay guest houses are rarely located on nude beaches and even if they are close by one, you still have to wear something to get back and forth. Taking an all-nude vacation can be tough to arrange, especially if you like to eat and the guest house you're staying in serves only breakfast and expects you to be dressed for the occasion.

If you are planning a trip with the objective of spending time nude, the most important criteria is – what are you actually looking for: nude sunbathing and swimming; a place where nudity sometimes occurs and is unofficially winked at; or a true clothing-optional experience? If the differences don't seem obvious when you're making your reservations, they will when you are at the resort and everyone else is dressed, or undressed, in the exact opposite of what you expected. It happens a lot. For the record, clothing-optional means that nudity is permitted throughout the entire accommodation, including buildings and grounds.

The clothing policy at heterosexual-oriented nudist resorts is clearly understood – you get to go nude everywhere all the time. Some gay resorts have similar policies and fortunately the number is growing, but most gay accommodations that permit nudity restrict it to designated areas. At those resorts, unless you spend your entire stay around the pool or hot tub, you'll wear clothes most of the time.

When making your reservations, the questions you should ask include:

Are you completely clothing-optional? If not, in what situations or areas is nudity permitted? It might be nice that a particular accommodation permits nudity in a fenced-in, three-man hot tub, but that does not a clothing-optional resort make. Those same resorts can sometimes be rigid about enforcing clothing requirements in all other public areas.

What meals do you serve and is dressing required for them? A number of truly clothing-optional resorts now serve three meals a day. At those resorts, you never have to get dressed or leave for anything unless you want to.

Are you limited to gay male guests only? Some guys find it awkward to share nudity with women. And first time guests arriving at a few resorts get surprised because those resorts advertise themselves as accommodating gay men, which they do, but conveniently leave out the fact that they also accommodate heterosexual couples.

How secluded are you? You wouldn't know it from their literature, but some places aren't very. Unless you are totally uninhibited, you can spend vacations at those resorts dashing from bush to bush while listening to cars and semi's whistle by on the four-lane about 50 yards away.

Will any special groups be there during my stay? Asking that question before you make a reservation will let you find out that you would be the only male at a lesbian gathering, or that the guest house will be hosting a NAMBLA convention that weekend. The latter event might get a little uncomfortable if you look about 18 and are still waiting for your chest hair.

You get the picture. Call and ask questions – even if you've been to a resort or guest house before. Ownership changes and so do attitudes. What was acceptable last year might be frowned on this year. Asking the right questions will let you spend your vacation dressed or undressed the way you want, not the way others are demanding.

If spending your entire visit nude is your primary objective, you should check out the gatherings for gay men held separately by IMEN and GNI each year (See their listings in the Organization Section). Those events are truly nude and they are attended by hundreds of men. The only clothing you'll see, even during meal time, is what's needed to ward off an evening chill or protect against sunburn. Local groups or clubs also host regional gatherings that have the same undress code. The IMEN quarterly newsletter generally has a complete listing of upcoming gatherings, or you can contact a club in your area to see what they may be planning.

When you do arrive at a new place, particularly a nude beach, it's a good idea to inquire locally to be sure that neither anti-nudity laws nor enforcement policies have changed. Perhaps the best rule of thumb is to not be the first person to go nude unless you are certain it is acceptable. If you are traveling internationally, remember, attitudes, laws and enforcement vary greatly from country to country. In some countries, anti-nudity laws can be quite restrictive and the punishments for breaking them can be quite severe. Use caution and good judgment.

TOURS AND TRAVEL

The Naked Travel Agent (TNTA)

The Naked Travel Agent is a reliable agent that specializes in gay destinations of all sorts. TNTA can assist you on any listing you may find in this guide.

Whether you have a specific destination in mind or just pre-planning, TNTA can help you decide based on your expectations for the perfect nude getaway. TNTA is discreet and can make you feel very comfortable in discussing your nude travel needs. TNTA's tehelphone number is (213) 656-8181 or by fax at (213) 656-8270.

Tour Operators

Tour operators that specialize in trips to areas where nude activity is possible include:

ARIZONA

Reservations Systems International
3819 North 3rd Street
Phoenix, AZ 85012
(800) 621-6503
(602) 263-1151
(602) 263-1153/FAX

Arranges complete package tours to the South Pacific including Australia and New Zealand.

FLORIDA

Fantasy World Tours
701 West Las Olas Blvd.
Ft. Lauderdale, FL 33312
(800) 771-1777
(305) 463-3911

Tours, cruises and travel arrangements to London, Athens/Mykonos, Amsterdam, Istanbul, Costa Rica, Israel, the Caribbean and Rio de Janeiro. Arranges both scheduled tours and independent travel.

Up Up and Away Travel
701 East Broward Blvd.
Fort Lauderdale, FL 33316
Ask for Tom
(305) 523-4944
(800) 234-0841

Arranges scheduled tours to Mykonos and Athens and Brazil. Tours include trips to nude beaches.

Tour Operators

NEW YORK

Odysseus
P. O. Box 1548
Port Washington, NY 11050
(516) 944-5330
(516) 944-7540/FAX

Tours and travel arrangements to Greece and the Greek Islands, Spain and the Canary Islands, France and St. Barts. Affiliated with the "Odyessus" Guide.

A listing in this section does not indicate or imply that the travel agency or tour operator, or any employee of the travel agent or tour operator condones or encourages nude activity. Rather, the firms are listed because of their ability to make travel arrangements to the destinations indicated.

Naked Magazine

As the name *Naked* suggests, this hot new magazine explores the sensual side of male nudity, filling a niche in the gay market that was previously unrecognized. And what a niche it must be, judging by the magazine's rapidly expanding print runs. *Naked* started out about two years ago as a rough, black and white publication that came out whenever. Now it's a slick, four-color, magazine that come out every five weeks and it is expected to become a monthly by the fall of 1995.

The magazine contains gay naturist news items and listing and a lot more. There are photo spreads, tid-bits and photos of interesting nude male activities from around the world, and page after page of personal letters from readers describing their own experiences.

Naked Magazine's sensual focus may differ from what many feel is appropriate for the naturist movement and that's fine. The magazine has not positioned itself as representing the movement.

Naked Magazine is available on most gay friendly newsstands, or you can subscribe to it at the following address: NAKED MAGAZINE SUBSCRIPTIONS, 7985 Santa Monica Blvd., #109-232, West Hollywood, CA 90046.

Nudist Organizations

Organized social nudity for gays is a relatively recent phenomena. But naturism as a movement has been around for a long time. For those who are interested, there are several national naturist organizations that promote naturism and and look after its interests. In many parts of the country there are local clubs that serve as social outlets for gay male naturists.

IMEN

IMEN – International Men Enjoying Naturism, Inc. – is a new organization on the gay naturist scene. But don't let its newness fool you. It was organized and is being run by a strong group of gay naturist veterans and it is expanding its membership base at a fast pace. If IMEN continues as it has, it will have a strong, positive effect on gay naturism.

Among other activities, IMEN publishes a quarterly newsletter, *The Naturist Gay-zette*, and it hosts annual international gatherings. Its newsletter is unusually comprehensive – the Spring 1995 issue was 48 pages – and it gives the best run-down on naturist club activities, nude tid-bits, and anything else that affects naturism, straight or gay.

Its first annual gathering will be held in mid-July, 1995 in Maryland, about the time this goes to press. They are expecting up to five hundred gay male naturists for a week in the sun.

You can contact them for membership information at:

IMEN, Inc.
P. O. Box 77122
Atlanta, GA 30357-1122
(404) 876-3064

NUDIST ORGANIZATIONS

G.N.I.

G.N.I. – Gay Naturists International – is the older of the gay naturist organizations. It has been through a series of changes over the past year or two, but remains active. It hosts an annual gathering in Pennsylvania each year. Previous gatherings have been attended by up to six hundred gay male naturists.
You can contact them for membership information at:

>G.N.I.
>324 Main Street, Suite 201
>Norwalk, CT 06851

The Naturist Society

The Naturist Society has long been in the forefront of the naturism movement. Headquartered in Oshkosh, Wisconsin the society publishes a magazine, *Nude and Natural*, and it also sells the popular *Lee Baxandall's World Guide to Nude Beaches & Recreation*. The society is supportive of gay naturist activities and it has at least one gay-oriented special interest group (SIG).

The society's membership is open to anyone and includes individuals, clubs and free beach associations. For membership information, you can contact them at:

>The Naturist Society
>P. O. Box 132
>Oshkosh, WI 54902
>(414) 426-5009
>(414) 231-9977 FAX

NUDIST ORGANIZATIONS 73

Gay Naturist Clubs

Gay naturist clubs form and fade away with regularity. The total number though seems to keep growing. A current list of gay naturist clubs (as accurate as we can make it given the frequency of changes) follows this section, and the individual clubs are also listed in the geographic section of this guide. If you contact a club by mail, there are two rules you should follow: use their acronyms, especially if the address is an individual's residence, and always enclose a business-sized self addressed stamped envelop.

American Association for Nude Recreation

The American Association for Nude Recreation (AANR) is the oldest naturist organization. Its membership is made up mostly of landed clubs and non-landed or traveling clubs. Membership in most of its clubs is limited by a quota system that attempts to ensure a gender balance. Normally, only 10% of club members can be single males. The balance is usually 80% couple and 10% single females.

You can contact them for membership information at:

American Association for Nude Recreation
1703 North Main Street
Kissimmee, Florida 34744
(407) 933-2064

The editors recommend that you join one of the gay naturist organizations and The Naturist Society. Besides providing information, that national organizations serve as watchdogs for legislative and law enforcement activities that would adversely affect naturism, especially on public beaches where nude sunbathing has historically been designated or permitted. The organizations can do their job better and protect your access to nude recreation with your support.

NOTES

Please Send Any Information That You May Have About Clothing Optional Accommodations, Beaches, Activities and Organizations.

By doing so, you'll help make the next edition of the Guide more useful for us all.

Please note corrections to a current listing or information about a potential new listing. The information we need includes:

Location including name and address if it is an accommodation, activity operator or organization:

_____
_____

Description, *i.e.*, nude beach, organization, resort, guest house, charter operator, tour operator, etc:

_____
_____

Description of facilities, beach, or activity - what are its assets, or what does it have to offer:

_____
_____
_____

How do you get to it - particularly if it is a beach or recreational area:

_____
_____
_____

Please use another sheet of paper for additional information or comments.

Send to: Summers Edge Studios, Inc.
           757 S.E. 17th Street, Suite 307
           Fort Lauderdale, FL 33316
           USA

ORDER FORM

Please mail or call if you would like to receive;

_____ A brochure showing Summers Edge Studio's other products and services.

_____ To order more copies of The World-Wide Guide to Gay Nude Resorts, Beaches & Recreation. See price list below.

	Guide Price List	Shipping & Handling
United States	$14.95	$2.00
Canada	$19.95	$2.50
Australia	$21.95	$2.50
New Zealand	$29.95	$3.00

NAME_____

ADDRESS_____

CITY & STATE_____

POSTAL CODE_____ COUNTRY_____

Send with check or money order, if applicable. Prices are guaranteed only until December 31, 1995. Send to:

Summers Edge Studios, Inc.
757 S.E. 17th Street
Fort Lauderdale, FL 33316
USA
(305) 764-6162

Credit Card Callers
(800) 488-6162
Accepting VISA, MC, AMEX, DISCOVER